D1607899

MY CONTRIBUTION TO
Collective
Consciousness

By A Nonspeaking
Autistic Speller

Cristofer Puleo

Table of Contents

FOREWORD 7

INTRODUCTION AND ACKNOWLEDGEMENTS 11

SECTION I

TOPICS IN ALPHABETICAL ORDER 17

SECTION II

CRISTOFER ANSWERS QUESTIONS ABOUT HIMSELF 103

SECTION III

APPENDIX 135

DEDICATION

This book is dedicated to my mom and my communication partner, Susanne Cannella.

It would not have been possible without both special women in my life.

FOREWORD

Cristofer is a 30-year-old nonspeaking man with autism. He had no means of communication until he was 23 years old. He started with the Rapid Prompting Method (RPM) and learned to use a letterboard to point to letters to make words and sentences. He is now in a program which uses Spelling to Communicate (S2C). More information about these similar methods is in the Appendix.

Collective consciousness refers to the set of shared beliefs, ideas, attitudes, and knowledge that are common to a social group or society. The collective consciousness informs our sense of belonging and identity, and our behavior. In this book, Cristofer reveals his contribution to society with his opinions on life's principles. He will also tell you about himself.

This book was developed over a period of years when his communication partner read to him classic fiction and non-fiction books and then asked him questions to solicit his opinion on the issues. It is obvious that he has strong opinions and great knowledge.

The book is divided into three sections:

Section 1 is arranged by topic in alphabetical order. It is best not to read it as you would a typical book, but rather go to a topic that interests you and ponder that category.

Section 2 is a collection of questions that Cristofer answers about himself. While people with autism are quite different from one another, there may be some similarities so this may be particularly interesting to parents who have nonspeaking autistic children.

Section 3 is the Appendix with helpful information about spelling as communication for autistics.

Cristofer is proud to be a cofounder of Crimsonrise, a neurodiverse community serving nonspeakers who, like Cristofer, desire access to communication.

Cristofer is also an artist and a few of his paintings are displayed throughout this book. The cover is one of his paintings titled *Collective Consciousness*.

Cristofer can be contacted by email:
Cristoferpuleo@gmail.com

These are entirely Cristofer's thoughts, and he spelled every word in this book except this Foreword and the Appendix.

Soft Night Silence

By Cristofer Puleo

INTRODUCTION and ACKNOWLEDGEMENTS

I wrote this book because I have the desire to inform, inspire and advocate for all nonspeakers in hopes that others will believe in our intelligence. Autism is a body/mind disconnect. My greatest challenge is controlling my body to do what I want it to do. My mind totally understands everything. Therefore, it is difficult to include myself in a world that doubts my intelligence just by looking at my actions. I actively listen to the help that guides me from within, which allows me to face this challenge.

I believe that the purpose of life is to know that God has created all with a purpose and a plan and that we are all one; part of one existence. We are here to learn from one another and to pass along our story to the next generation. Our lives are all connected, each affects the other and all our questions will be answered in the journey beyond here. God will show you the purpose of your existence and you will come to find all the lessons learned here.

Each of my thoughts offers something for everyone. You may not agree with all, but within this book there are some that may be relatable. These thoughts capture who I am, and I am glad to finally communicate confidently the truth about me, giving friends hope to tell their truth too.

My hope is for the world to gain humanity and inclusion, joining together as one diversified nation with equality and a better understanding of one another.

I want to thank all my angels on earth and above who have supported me. I am grateful for my family and friends, and the many teachers, therapists and aides who have helped me throughout my life. Nick D'Amora, you opened the door and led me and so many others to a world of communication. Thank you for being my mentor and friend. Tejas, another special friend, you are the strength and support I rely upon. You are a fierce advocate and I admire your courage and wisdom. Mary Giorgio and Eileen Cunningham, thank you for always having faith in me and giving me opportunities to mentor others. Susanne Cannella, thank you for presuming my competence and spending hours reading to me and asking me questions so that I could express my opinions which formed the basis of this book. Mom and dad, you are my beating heart.

With love, *Cristofer*

Fields of Autumn

by Cristofer Puleo

SECTION I
Topics in alphabetical order

AGING

I look at aging in terms of educational growth. I want to learn more, do more, see more and experience more. For me, aging is bringing my soul closer to God to fulfill a mission on teaching others' acceptance.

Some people are unhappy about aging because their lives are unfulfilled and lack purpose.

There is discrimination against the elderly in our society especially in times when they are disabled or sick. Life is celebrated when one is productive and engaging. Some people have grand egos, believing in their power over the weak and they deliver disrespect and intimidation, controlling others' spirits because they decided the elderly are no longer a functioning representation of society.

Aging for men is difficult mostly due to the loss of the physical abilities they once had. For women, insecurities arise with age over losing their physical youthful appearance.

ANGELS

Angels to me means carriers of spirit, intending to strengthen one's own spirit. They also deliver God's messages. There are many forms of angels and not the symbolic kind you think of. There are times they speak to us, those times when there are no explanations, those times when situations seem too convenient. They intervene with our energy. Often you can tune in and you will hear them.

ANGER

Anger will not be a solution to any problem. Patience and time are the answer.

Anger attacks from within, a slow and steady pain. In its way compassion struggles to be released. Anger begins to wear on the spirit and hardens the soul. Let it go. No one is born with anger.

I am tuned into people's energy all the time. For me, anger is a difficult energy to handle, making trouble for my heart.

Anger is an unstabilizing emotion. It will paralyze the love within and block one from receiving all healthy emotions needed for growing one's soul.

ANIMALS

I find God in all creatures which are created here for a purpose. The intention always is to provide a relationship bound to humans. Animals are purposeful friends.

Most animals give unconditional love, always a companion at your side. I feel less lonely and comforted by their company. Also, they have a sense about you unlike any other. They rise to meet your emotional needs and give you a sense of responsibility to care for something other than yourself.

Dogs sense energy. They are aware of things through their senses. I certainly believe they understand our emotions and can sense environmental forces. Each animal is unique in their sensory abilities. Dogs address human emotions and energy with more understanding.

Dogs teach people to allow unconditional love.

Dogs and animals have spirits. I believe all energy is part of the plan here; all are created and given back to God. Souls are what connects us

From long ago dogs have had the ability to relate to live amongst a pack. They are easily trainable and easy to live with emotionally. They serve as friends, loyal and kind to their pack. This is an instant gratification for humans' emotional needs

Birds are God's messengers. They have a history long before we arrived and are symbolic to many cultures.

Finding a dead bird is not always bad but may indicate having something in your life end. Finding a bird's nest is the opposite - a change of something new in your life.

Crows are a very intelligent species of birds. Crows have the ability to solve problems. They find sources of food and shelter and at times can trick humans to serve for their own survival benefit.

Pigs in nature are very intelligent and can be seen as having human traits as far as rationalizing and problem solving.

I consider all animals instinctively wise. Horses have always been intelligent and have survived many years. I find them keenly sensitive and intuitive with a docile manner that makes them interesting.

Live heartily to provide caring support for all that share this earth. I believe it is God's ideology to protect all living creatures from extinction and involve people to continue balancing life on earth.

Animals take only what they need for food, shelter, and biological needs. They don't overeat or make enormous homes. They balance their lives to be happy, peaceful, and comfortable.

I am not opposed to the idea of hunting to satisfy the need to eat and survival. I am opposed in doing it for sport.

Treat the world first with dignity and respect. Pay close attention to the destruction our carelessness causes. Treat animals respectfully. Protect their habitats. Refrain from hunting without purpose. Overall, make the earth livable. Treat it as a gift and serve to protect it.

I am against any idea of poaching. I don't see the need to destroy a life, and possibly an entire species for human selfishness.

Everyone can benefit by serving and caring for others or for animals and nature. Taking care of someone or something other than yourself can bring joy and satisfaction to your soul.

APPEARANCES

Don't discount another based upon appearance. Be aware we all are not what we appear to be. We are recognized wrongly for our physical bodies. We allow appearances to come first in our relationships with others and then underestimate the abilities that go deeper. We need to make adjustments to those ideas.

Don't misjudge or assume one is not capable just because they look weak or are lacking physical strength or coordination. Outside appearances never truly represent the beauty that may lie within.

It's unfortunate that most of the younger generation has put the most emphasis on physical appearances. It's even more upsetting to see many still holding value to this as they get older.

I believe the outside physical appearances matter to many, and some need that extrinsic beauty to make themselves happy. No one is to blame; it is culturally demanding.

Scars are reminders of our past and our physical flaws create our own uniqueness and sense of identity. It's courageous and empowering to accept imperfections and to focus on creating self-esteem in other ways.

ART

Art is the subconscious mind between what is reality and each emotional aspect of thought.

I am one to seek inspiration by the visual beauty that surrounds me. These concepts, such as art, speak without words. Art evokes emotion, something I have a keen sense about. It allows all to embrace the experience without judgement or pressure.

My art captures my spirit resonance and emotion. It is made to make one feel the movement and flow of the paint.

AUTISM

When I think of the word spectrum (as in autism spectrum), I envision a beautiful rainbow, one with vibrant and distinct colors; each one unique yet sharing in the same exhilarating experience. Struggles exist for everyone. We wouldn't be human without them. However, our lives need fulfillment with hope and faith; not a life of what is difficult or not possible but rather seeing abilities and opportunities… like a rainbow supported by each color to fill up a dreary sky.

Man has invented toxins and spoiled the world. There are just too many for autistic bodies to handle.

I am challenged by my eyes focusing. Reading words is like seeing pictures in my head. I can determine the words by putting them together with visual representation.

Most people manage to make eye contact and it comes relatively easy for them. Autistics are challenged mostly by the coordination to do this. They may feel intimidated too, but for most, it's the lack of skill that inhibits us from making eye contact.

Many think we must be focused when we listen. The truth is, I am listening all the time. I interrupt other facets of communication to listen to more prominent conversations or more important information.

I greatly appreciate when I am spoken to directly. It is challenging for some to just talk to me, even when I am alone with them. It seems easier when more people are involved.

All parents of autistic children worry what will become of their children when they leave this earth. They worry that the guardianship may not be suitable. This is part of my worry too. I have faith that my life will be granted the support I need to live without my mom or dad.

My advice to parents of autistic children starting this journey is to forget everything you have heard, everything you have learned and everything you have tried in regard to helping your child's autism. Going further now, interest yourself in guiding and supporting your child's resistant motor function and providing them faith in their ability to succeed.

I always heard people mention the term "low functioning". It is sad to hear autistics called this.

I don't like the word disability. Rather, use the phrase people with differences.

If I was to write another commandment, I would add: Thou shall know that all autistics can learn.

All siblings whether they have a brother or sister with autism or not will find that there will be battles for attention. However, having an autistic sibling can be enriching, teaching one the value of being compassionate.

Q: What would you say to all the critics who discredit this method of spelling to communicate (S2C)?

A: First tell me are you faithful in believing that blind people can read or that crippled people can travel? This letter board is my braille, is my wheelchair, is my motor support and necessary accommodation to communicate.

Q: What would you say to another nonspeaker who is about to start the journey with S2C?

A: Allow the senses to let down their guard. Kind hearts are about to fulfill your dreams. Understand when learning you will need patience. Find your inner strength. Make every effort. I promise you a way of communication is about to transpire when your regulated body is given this opportunity.

Q: What are your thoughts about the research being done in the S2C field?

A: I'm afraid it's not convincing for this is not easily seen as independent to some. Some will deny us getting our education with incorporating the letter board because we are not able to hold the board and coach our motor all at once. It is best to allow time to guide those who already have an open mind, rather than trying to convince those constrained by uncertainty.

BULLYING

Bullying can end if we teach love.

Never let someone's title or authority overpower you. Stand up to those who bully or use aggression to take you down. Mindful strategies can be just as forceful.

Intimidation is the goal of a bully. Overpower them with the strength of confidence. Love people no matter their flaws. Hearts filled are stronger than those that are empty.

CHRISTMAS

Christmas is the love for a child, the sacrifices parents make, the pureness of giving while asking nothing in return, and the love brought to us the very first Christmas day through our Savior Jesus Christ. God is the gift at Christmas and all the love that comes from Him to us.

Giving Santa a title gives children the wrong impression of Christmas. A real story about gifts of love would be more suitable. Christmas has been more about materials over the years and less about giving love and service to others.

Christmas is a nice feeling of love. In my experience, I am more in tune with the sounds of Christmas. Music and bells and songs are all gifts to my ears at Christmas.

COMPETITION

Competitiveness can measure one's self-worth when comparing to others. It's challenging for one not to be competitive. As humans, we absorb it to be accepted. We place great emphasis on competition in our world - from money, jobs, appearance, sports, education. All are pressured to compete.

We are made to emulate and celebrate being inspired by others. I am pleased by my own individual achievements. Friends are my inspiration, not my competition.

DEATH

Cherish your loved one in your heart. Their love lives on. They are in your thoughts, memories and when you think of them, they will be there. Thinking of a loved one who has passed on brings that person close. Focus on that love between you and there you will find them. Ask God to talk to them. You can hear them if you listen closely. The physical world distracts. Carefully listen. It's God's way of helping you heal. Celebrate their life and not mourn their passing. They are not gone. An eternity of peace and love await them.

A goodbye is never forever. Souls never truly leave. We are all made of energy and that never dies. In spirit we shall remain one. A farewell to this body but not a goodbye to this soul; only say have a nice journey.

Acceptance of life is death, to accept life one must accept death. Energy doesn't stop. Death does not exist amongst the spirits. Death is just an event of life, a conclusion, but not an end. Celebrate death because it's a completion of life, a graduation and a mastering of another journey. All continue on finding their way closer to God. I am loving death as much as I am loving life. Fear nothing about it. Devote your sadness of losing friends or family to the empowerment and glorification of their spirit and their new journey ahead.

One day all will become one with the stars.

Your guardian angel comes to get you when you die. All have special angels that help and assist us to cross over when it is our time to ascend life into another field of learning.

In thinking of my deceased relatives, I find comfort in knowing they are loved and included in spiritual harmony, supported by God's love, beginning a new home.

Those we love, God has connected us for specific reasons, to teach us while we are here. The love never leaves, it's eternal, embedded in our hearts. Consider this each time you think of your loved one. Mourning a mortal life but gaining another angel... a return home. God has called them back. They are not gone. Although unheard and unseen, their love will always be given. It is necessary to believe with your heart. It's faith that joins our spirits. Celebrate in love, not in mourning. Appreciate all the love given and all that is yet to be gained. Call upon these moments to help you heal your sorrow.

We have an abundant number of friends in the afterlife. We are given a home there, a completed home.

When one faces final days, it leaves you vulnerable to see what is truly important in life.

If people knew they were going to die, almost all would face mistakes and manage their contributions to life in a more generous and compassionate way. Some people hold on before they pass away especially if there are unresolved conflicts or if the family struggles to let their spirit free. They are often given the choice to stay or go back. If their mission is complete, they are not given the choice.

I often feel the spirits of family who have passed on. They do not tell me who they are, but I sense they are my family; a familiar energy of spirits I have known.

All funerals are stationed with sadness and those who have passed are not there to witness the cherished affection. It is best if you could compose a celebration for them while they are alive to recognize their contributions in this life.

I believe the spirit is aware of when we will pass on.

Q: What are your thoughts on people who die young?

A: All spirits are brought together in this life for a reason, fulfilling a purpose, celebrating the gifts each brings to our lives. It is a commitment to God to live for others more than yourself. Lives are meant to teach others. Spirits are fulfilled when this commitment has expired, and it does not matter the age. All are equal.

Q: Do you believe any crime should be punishable by death?

A: All life is sacred. Some make faulty choices, but God gives His mercy. It is not a decision humans should make.

Q: Do you believe that objects can contain the energy of spirits who are no longer here?

A: If you lay upon them, seeing that spirit, reliving memories and placing all loving energy into it, it can bring forth the energy of that spirit. Like prayers, energy is strong enough to be heard.

Q: What are your thoughts about the Buddhist philosophy... live every day asking yourself is this the day I die?

SECTION I: TOPICS IN ALPHABETICAL ORDER

A: Better to say this is the day I live. Life is not truly ending so to say this is the day I live gives the opportunity for the soul to start a new way if one is needed.

<u>Mourning Prayer by Cristofer</u>

Heavenly Savior
Halo surrounds the loving glory
Of your Spirit.
Mourning a loss never forgotten
Lifted above in your honor
Praying hearts eternally united

DEPRESSION

Someone with depression needs a person who will just listen to him, someone who is understanding and non-judgmental and who will affirm their feelings; someone who will support their emotions without managing or criticizing.

Loving something in your life can distract sadness.

Putting effort into helping others will bring satisfaction to your soul.

DIVERSITY

I am respectful of both similarities and differences of all people. Accepting this gives us the opportunity to learn from one another. If we were all the same there would be no spiritual growth. Our uniqueness is how we grow, expand, and join together on a mission of support and development in creating a human bond cared for by God.

I believe people want to hear and see their views in others. It makes them comfortable, secure and in control. Truth is something people have a challenge identifying.

Sharing common interests helps spread the love and supports your ideas, which makes one joyful and content. However, learning from individual differences makes one appreciate the uniqueness in us all.

EDUCATION AND LEARNING

I'm a believer in both education and hard work. Education is a great gift but to profit from it, one should consider how important it is that we apply our strengths and abilities. Not much gets accomplished without hard work.

Having any opportunity to learn for me is a reward. I seek this opportunity in my life for it is a goal of every human to experience an education and to empower ourselves with knowledge.

All should be given the same educational opportunities. When one is struggling, then extra support should be given to help him learn.

Education should embrace a humanistic approach, remembering the emotional and spiritual well-being of the students.

Give everyone an equal opportunity to be heard. You never know what you may learn.

I find many people, especially young adults and teens, struggle to find their own identity. I am discovering it's a learning process all must go through.

The world never stops teaching. It's our responsibility to never stop learning. Giving up on knowledge means giving up on your dignity, your reasons to live.

Learning is not only through books or text. Learning involves the senses through experiences. It resonates within our hearts, not just our minds. More is taught within our worldly encounters than lectures. The gift is when we share our learning with others.

All must learn to embrace change. It's our only chance at growth.

God's plan for all is continuous learning and discovering. Life is a learning journey. Love is the way to win.

Our comfort zone is the protection we give ourselves, the reason we do what we do, all based around our level of comfort. Each time I celebrate something learned, some new experience I am involving my comfort zone. I have gone beyond this zone when I first began communicating my thoughts. It is comforting, of course, to stay within the zone, but not expanding the boundaries allows the spirit to starve itself of knowledge. Restricting the soul of experience hinders the opportunities of learning.

EMPATHY/EMPATH

(Many people with autism have high empathy skills and as such are empaths. Cristofer speaks about being an empath.)

Q: What are your thoughts about being an empath?

A: I am blessed every day. I consider this one of my many gifts. I am not challenged by my empathy. I accept and appreciate it and use it to help others. However, it is a challenge to be an autistic empath. Often the chance to work on strategies is disrupted by my body and not always the opportunity to say how you are feeling and what support you may need. I am greatly healed when I talk (via spelling). It releases my energy troubles.

Q: What are some advantages of being an empath?

A: I want to heal others all the time. I only want love and peace and to help others always live a happy life. I am frustrated when others are feeling more with their minds than their hearts.

Q: What is a common challenge to being an empath?

A: Energy consumes you. You often have compassion fatigue.

Q: What makes overloaded symptoms worse?

A: Being around negative people.

Q: What improves sensory overload?

A: Meditation is great for me.

Q: Which emotions from others affect you the most?

A: I am affected by all energies. I am definitely intoxicated by anxiety. Certainly, I am happy to feel all positive energy, but I am troubled by non-loving energy.

Q: The anxiety you feel, is it often your own or another's?

A: You ask an important question. I believe it is more another's anxiety that most affects my own anxiety.

Q: Does proximity to another's energy field have more significance?

A: Energy is felt at all distances; always stronger within close proximity.

Q: Can that energy last upon the empath throughout the day, even after a person leaves the space?

A: A strong energy will go on for quite some time. An extensive amount can last all week.

Q: What are your thoughts about protective strategies?

A: It is best for all to take care by avoiding toxic people, especially when that person's negative emotional energy is high.

Q: What is your most sensitive point for feeling toxic energy?

A: My gut and head feel discomfort from toxic energy.

Q: How does the energy of physical space and objects affect an empath?

A: Definitely I am greatly affected by surrounding energy due to physical space and objects. It is best to be in large open areas as close to nature as possible. Artificial light hides good energy flow. I am affected by energy from all sources although physical and object energy remain a constant; it's not as draining as emotional energy shared by people.

Q: Why do empaths suffer from emotional contagion?

A: All are connected by a binding force. Some are more sensitive to this energy than others. Emotions travel easily through this central force and are felt intensely by empaths. It's a lot like you being joyful when your children are successful at something new and you take on not only your own joy, but the joyous energy they emit as well.

Q: What is an energy vampire?

A: People who are attracted to a loving energy and will only use it for their own advantage.

Q: Why is it difficult for an empath to identify a narcissist?

A: They have a heart filled with love and a mindset that all other people share the same. It is difficult for empaths to imagine that the gift of love is not found in others' hearts.

EQUALITY

I believe the country still struggles with equality and people are afraid to accept their prejudices and misunderstandings about differences in us all.

I measure people based upon the love, faith, and belief that I feel from their hearts.

All need to know the importance of inclusion. When included you feel a sense of belonging and it promotes a positive approach on your self-esteem. Being accepted increases opportunities for friendships which help overall life experiences.

EUTHANASIA

I believe life is in the hands of God. To end it out of discomfort does the spirit a disservice. To induce death of the body creates a stalling as the spirit embarks on the next journey. It is fine to make one comfortable and support their pain or struggle. I believe it is not man's place to intervene. I believe all spirits feel the time when it is ready to transition, this time of passing and God calling.

FAILURE

Mistakes provide the opportunity for correction and learning.

A mistake is all part of life's learning. Without mistakes there are no lessons and without lessons there is no progress, and if you can't progress then you can never succeed.

God did not make us perfect. He gives us a chance to improve and learn life's true story.

FAMILY

Family is important because it gives genuine support, comforting love and dependability. It is a bond unlike any other. Count on family to provide and protect every moment of your life.

A family is a commitment between parents and children. It is a bond never to be broken.

I'm afraid modern families have lost a commitment to their children. The values have shifted. A larger portion of time is spent here on work rather than with the true purpose of family. Also, the world has made it tough to spend time together. Everyone is so busy.

Parents need to nurture their children's spirits, focusing on having goodness rather than wealth.

Rivalry exists in every relationship, more so with children seeking the attention of their parents, since this is the first relationship experienced. Many are longing to make their parents pleased. Life is about acceptance.

Truth is important, especially to children, regarding who their parents and family's identities are.

Roots are important to preserve a past and to support tradition; to ground oneself to shape the future.

A lot of unhappy and dissatisfied people giving too much time to work and money and not enough time for family socializing. Give more time to love than work.

If a child only has one parent, I'm happy to say that family is also a very important role in a child's life. Grandparents, aunts and uncles all provide that balance and structure when there is that void.

All kids have one parent they rely on more than the other. Each child will look and search for love wherever they need it most. Each parent will give their love in different ways.

I find mothers to be the heart and soul of every family. Moms are appointed caregivers asked to guide us. So many have internal intuition. A mother's force to keep family together. Without a mother's presence family members drift apart.

All need their mother's love. For boys, it's the first love you know. Mothers are careful creators and nurturers to the soul. The bond is unlike any other to experience.

Families all leave messages for the generations that follow. Spirits never reach an end. They convey their stories through memories and an abundance of devotion even after the physical state has passed.

Families can get along even if their cultures and religions are different because the fact is, love sees beyond all differences.

I believe children are a gift meant to enhance life. They can affect families in various ways. They are a learning experience. Their presence can alter parents' goals but can also bring great emotional value.

Always teach a child through love, not anger. Accept their faults and allow them to manage and learn about their actions' consequences through non-abusive means.

Consider balancing both work and family. Invest in both but family must never lack support due to work. Family affairs come first.

Q: Do you believe that we are and can be different than our ancestors?

A: Absolutely. Each is uniquely created. Although similarities exist, individuality is amongst us. All change is also a possibility. Being aware of your families and their faults can lead one to change the course of their lives, just as one can choose to blame family's faults for their delinquencies.

Q: Do you think it's okay for parents to make decisions for their children?

A: This is not harmful but also as adults, there comes a freedom of choice. Not all adults have this freedom and rely on loved ones to make their choices, but for the ones who can, it is their individual choice that matters.

FEAR

Fear is the lowest vibration, the root of every problem. It causes blockage to energy flow, allowing the heart to become weak and if the heart is weak, one will be susceptible to more energy disturbances.

Fear and excitement are two emotions relatively similar. It can trick you sometimes. Both can have similar feelings manifested for different reasons with totally different outcomes.

When you manifest your fears, and put that energy into action, it then becomes environmentally absorbed. It will cycle through the environment and affect others as well as eventually cycle back to you. Void it by releasing the fearful thoughts immediately.

Don't let fear control your decisions. Allow yourself to face your fears. If you can't face anything scary or daunting, then you will never understand your strength or ability to rise above what limits you.

You have to slowly deal with fear, taking time to distance and reflect and not try to fight it. It serves a purpose, or it wouldn't be a feeling given from God. It's important we ask His help guiding us through fear, helping us learn ways to improve our spirit.

FOOD

I believe food prepared by someone you love has a feeling of care and comfort. There is an indescribable set of emotions attributed to food that evokes the senses and can bring pleasure to most.

Many in our society and culture are accustomed to eating for pleasure and not for the purpose of strength and well-being. Many do not value the source of their food and grossly indulge, managing to waste food as they do so.

I believe in the power of God's creations. All fruits, vegetables and herbs found in nature can have benefit to the body. It is always best when consumed straight from the earth. A great deal of energy and nutrients are from them uncooked, whole, and not processed with nothing additionally included. It is best having a healthy diet from God created food most of the time. Eating unhealthy foods can be a reward occasionally.

FORGIVENESS

Repenting and forgiveness are the two most powerful ways of life.

It takes a lot of love to forgive another. A great amount of love must be felt for oneself before forgiving another.

True remorse opens the soul.

Forgiveness brings peace. Forgive yourself, forgive others. It will free the soul allowing room for more positive growth and allowing the spirit happiness and compassion.

When you forgive it allows your heart to love more.

Forgiveness is a cleansing, a renewal of spirit. God has given us this gift and asks that we all use it.

FRIENDS

You can't force a friendship. It is a growth you can't create in a short time.

True friends are sometimes difficult to find. Best to have no friends than to have the wrong friends.

Friendships are love and the two cannot be separated. The gift of true friends is love.

Friendship is a strong, interpersonal bond built by strong values of love, loyalty, trust and respect for one another.

Friendship can neither be bought nor sold. It is a gift from God, cherished and adored.

Friends can be just as loving as family. Friends can guide you through life's challenges. Always know who your true friends are.

A good friend feels your feelings without you saying a word. Friends are your strength and love in good times as well as in bad times.

People need to connect to other people. Having trusted human relationships is essential to our well-being.

Life is not solitary. We are here to live together and offer help to ease each other's burdens and comfort each other when needed.

People need to know the importance of inclusion. When included, you feel a sense of belonging and it promotes a positive approach to your self-esteem. Being accepted increases opportunities for friendships which help overall life experiences.

God is so much like a friend, always loving.

GAMBLING

Gambling is an easy way to lose money.

GIVING

Giving charitable donations is honorable and admirable. It is in God's favor and His best interest to give back and keep giving. That is my idea of practicing my faith in God. Giving in love to those in need strengthens my values and morals overall, benefiting my soul and heart's contentment.

No matter how much money you earn, nothing is more rewarding than what we give. The soul's power to give to those in need is truly a rewarding gift for one's heart. Heal your heart through giving. In selfishness, one will never be satisfied.

Celebrate the gift of giving and your heart will receive tremendous love.

Everyone can benefit by serving and caring for others or for animals and nature. Taking care of someone or something other than ourselves can bring joy and satisfaction to your soul.

A real way to give is through the heart.

Favors are not contracts. Giving should come from the heart without seeking anything in return.

If you do something from love, you will never be dissatisfied. Offering your time, your help, your knowledge in unselfish ways serves a satisfied spirit.

If you are constantly giving of yourself, then you are blocking the path of receiving. Manage to find a balance… equal amount of input versus output.

GOVERNMENT

Our country is easily divided and torn by emotion. The freedom of speech makes it easy for us to manipulate and persuade others. If this persuasion manipulates the wrong minds, then it would continue to grow into a country overpowered by corruption allowing our rights and opportunities to be taken away.

I believe the United States can provide all necessities for itself but chooses to trade with other countries for economic gains and to be supportive to other countries.

Thankfully our country is one of democracy where the people have choice over their leaders. A good leader considers the needs of the people and joins them together, not tears them apart, and is careful not to intimidate the world.

We are fortunate to live in a country that provides for those who are limited to perform work, but I am afraid not every country offers the same support.

GROWTH

Change is our only chance at growth.

It is comforting, of course, to stay within your comfort zone, but not expanding the boundaries allows the spirit to starve itself of knowledge. Restricting the soul of experience hinders the opportunities of learning.

GUILT

When one lets go of guilt the soul becomes lighter, pushing a weight off a heavy heart.

Guilt locks the spirit from embracing love.

HAPPINESS

Happiness is found through achievements and experiences, both good and bad experiences. We go through our troubles in order to find happiness. Allowing happiness only after milestone goals are achieved, one will not always be happy; it's allotted through self-reward by the effort made.

Be a master of joy. Stop worrying.

I think it's important to be true to oneself, to reflect upon one's own spirit, to find self-happiness. Happiness will not come from a career, a place, or a person. Happiness can only come from one's own heart. Search within yourself. It's not far away.

Happiness is a choice. For me it is an easy choice because I can create my own happiness. Controlling inner happiness is not easy for most because they allow thoughts to con-sume their energy flow.

Throughout all events consider your commitment to happiness. Don't allow events to define or change your happiness. Make the choice within and create your soul's own standard of happiness.

Be humble, modest, confident and envision success. This will lead you on a path of true happiness.

The key to staying happy is keeping one's heart open; not allowing your inner energy to close or block the flow. Stay positive and calm. Release all negativity and all-consuming thoughts. Stay committed to being happy no matter what life may bring. Throughout it all, just have fun.

Our world is full of many intelligent people, and we are thankful to have advanced in so many ways. However, our world is still learning. I find there are many things still undiscovered and truthfully our nation still has a lot of healing to do. There is much hurt in the world. Happiness is misrepresented and misunderstood. Too many are exchanging money for happiness; too many vainly involved; too many caring only about themselves. We need to save our world through recognition and acts of kindness.

HEALING

Emotions can trigger physical unbalance. It can affect all systems and disrupt cycles.

Both happy and sad emotions can affect all physical systems and disrupt cycles.

Sick people are healed through happiness and positive support, not sadness and despair.

To heal, one must not remain hidden in the past, but to look towards a future of promise, purpose, and hope.

If your heart is at peace, your body will remain healthy. Realize all people have powers within themselves to heal the body. Pray to God. Keep Him in your prayers of healing.

HOME

It's the love felt that makes a house a home.

Always have room for privacy and a place that is comforting to all. It's best to seek some individual time alone.

HOPES and DREAMS

Always mention your hopes and dreams out loud. It is effective when they are heard. If love is surrounded by these hopes, then it will be supported. Always believe in the power of love and the will to make your dreams become a reality.

HOW TO LIVE

Focus on what you can do today, not tomorrow. Life is meant to be lived in the moment. Many bring upon unnecessary stress when they live in the past or focus on the future.

If everyone only stopped to listen, it's the most powerful human sense. Not many know or can unlock its true strength. Sight can blur its worth. Isolating the sense of hearing will bring truth to its potential.

More emotion is seen through the eyes than any other facial feature. Realize the eyes speak the truth.

Neutralize negativity with love.

If we knew our challenges ahead of time, we would have no way of assessing our strength. Some would fight defeat and accept challenges while others choose to run. A spontaneous challenge is a gift, a test from God to determine your faith, your courage, your spirit's bravery, and reliance. Life is set up for accepting challenges.

Most people see what they want to see, what they have been told to see, and preconceived ideas that have been taught to them. Their expectations come from conventional wisdom. This does not open the mind and spirit to miracles and life's surprises that can change the way one observes the world.

Life is not made to live alone but rather one needs to have a network of support from friends, family and even the kindness of strangers. You have to rely on others in this world.

Approach life with an open heart.

It is not our job, our responsibility to change the world, but we can choose to change ourselves, which can have influence upon others. Go through the motions one step at a time.

Believe in good and good will come to you. Always keep faith in God and trust in His plan. Keep believing in others and believe in yourself.

Listen and feel with your heart.

All comes around when it is supposed to. Intend for it to occur naturally. Giving too much pressure will force negative energy upon it. Relax, stay calm and let love shine upon it. Ask that happiness surround us. Make one decision at a time. Step aside and allow an open flow. Release tension and relax. Listen to the powers around you. They will guide.

A bad habit is hard to break, and good habits will not break you.

There is no sin in fun, as long as it's innocent fun.

Comparing yourself stops you from gaining knowledge intended to grow your soul.

You must have your own guidance. This leads to your destiny.

Don't admire anyone to the point where it would change who you are.

Never give up. Always have hope. Love will find you. No need to search for it. God has left it inside all of us.

In life, there are challenges and people you will meet that can change your directional path. Through all struggles, one must never overlook the spark of hope in every direction.

Birthday...don't celebrate just for the day, but everyday celebrate the reason you are here.

Don't ever assume that others have better lives than yours.

All we want and find important is right in front of us.

We should make our life choices upon how we can serve and grow and by experiences we gain from our choices to empower our spirits.

It is best to focus only on the good or positive aspects of your life.

One gains knowledge through accidents and mistakes. Learn from life's experiences whether they bring troubling encounters or joyful occasions.

Accept what you have, cherish, and love all that surrounds you. One never knows when all you ever have is gone. Live in the moment, focus on the present, let hopes and dreams guide you but never lose sight of what's in front of you.

Humans have a great fear of being alone

Always stop to see the beauty God put in front of us.

A good habit for healthy living is to stay positive.

Beware of the power of taking the wrong advice.

Spoil one with the heart and guide one with the head.

Stop worrying about what you don't have and go with what you do have.

Every life matters.

Dance can bring life to your spirit.

There is so much truth in the ying and yang. The ying and yang concept are two extremes in life. In order to have balance, one must not go to extremes. Find a center for harmony.

See misery…join misery
See joy…join joy

A smile is honest, loving and often genuine. The energy around frowns or furrowed brows is often difficult to deal with.

Life is about patience and the understanding that people go at their own pace. Accept those whose pace may be different than yours.

Take time to reflect on what will make a difference. Don't look for the easy way out.

To build character, learn from your experiences and be humble, loving and generous.

Talk with your heart and listen with your soul.

Those who are shallow will never find the comfort of being emotionally satisfied.

Life needs both ups and downs. Find them equally challenging. Rising to the top requires the same mind, same thoughtfulness. You can't let it change your thinking. You need to still be mindful and careful avoiding conflict or mistakes, keeping yourself humble. Have appreciation whether you make it to the top or get knocked down to the bottom. Regardless of the outcome, it's the climb and one's attitude that truly matters.

Living is more than a physical state. Life is happening all around us. Accept life everywhere, not just for your own spirit, but a purpose for all. Learn from living. Face the pain. Love is eternal. It demands sacrifice. We must make these sacrifices for spiritual evolution for the next generation. We leave our love with them as we carry on to the glory quest to meet the existence of God.

Each life has a purpose, so realize its potential but also recognize its limitations. Serve your time here well and accept service. When it's over here, this service will continue. Treat life as eternal, with a great reward for missions completed with trust, love, and honor.

I believe social media can be harmful and promotes unhappiness. It's the same with the news. It gives people a false sense of hope, mixed signals, and misrepresented messages. Also, it is dangerous to our youth who are still impressionable. Unfortunately, you can't avoid it either.

It is ok to cry for yourself and for others.

Approach life with an open heart.

Honesty is a virtue of life. It's more than just telling the truth. It speaks volumes about your integrity and the ability to live sincerely. Live a genuine and trustworthy life.

One can only change if they want to change. Many change to suit the needs of others. The only way to make a difference is to change for yourself.

Be observant of all the beauty that surrounds you, the purpose of your life, the reason you are here, the joys life has brought, and the gifts awarded to your spirit.

You can't find peace within your own heart if you are constantly disrupted by the lives of others. Find your own journey, your own goals. Invest in self-reflection. You are the keeper of your life. Trust in God to see you through.

Singing touches upon the soul. You can feel it with your heart. If you are connected spiritually, then singing can evoke emotion of being overjoyed by a beautiful voice.

Sometimes you should find a way to mend the past first before moving forward. The spirit realizes there is something puzzling our life that still needs time to learn.

When people feel threatened, anger and resentment build up and people become selfishly absorbed.

People need people in this life because the soul needs to feel the presence of other loving souls.

You can't be physically independent in everything you do so accept dependency without anger, embarrassment, or shame. Take comfort in it. It is learning to acclimate in a situation or experience you have been given.

Take what you need and replenish it with something new. Balance is created in the universe when voids are filled, and greed is lessened.

Balance the things that truly matter in life. Devote yourself to people, nature and learning life is everlasting. Live it with a loving heart. Find meaning and purpose in everything you do. Fulfill your time being thankful, grateful, and never think life doesn't matter.

All growth needs the opportunity for both joy and sorrow. We must experience every emotion in order to increase love and to overcome our fears. This is the greatest challenge of them all.

Reach enlightenment by knowing one's own identity and true self.

Always give clarity on your intentions.

Don't indulge yourself in too much of a good thing. It will leave you a glutton for punishment.

Kindness reaches the heart quicker than insensitivity.

Slow down, stop to acknowledge each moment, each emotion, and every experience. Stay conscious of your surroundings and those who have impact on your life. Give time to process and accept your alignment with the world. Be mindful of rest and health. Be present in the hands of God trusting and appreciating the gifts you have been given.

Q: What should be the main focus for us to live peacefully in our culture?

A: To become more aware of our potential to live and give equal opportunity; to consider one's strengths and help them with their weaknesses. The only way to rise up is to recognize but don't run from problems. Accomplish gains and believe, trust, and invest in the human family. Give love and people a chance.

Q: Should we be responsible for one another?

A: We need to be caring and supportive but not be responsible for someone else. Each takes their own responsibility. That is the way we test our learning.

Q: What are your thoughts about Earth?

A: Earth is a really difficult realm of consciousness. It is a place filled with so many extremes and levels of emotional energy. We are dependent on others for balance and support. Earth is a place where we need to learn how to manage our spirit in groups. This is definitely not easy. All are in conflict. Often agreement towards love is challenging.

JUDGEMENT

God is the only one who can judge. It's not man's responsibility. Judgement leads to separation of human civilization. It feeds hatred and destroys the spirit.

LAUGHTER

Smiles and laughter evoke genuine joy. To laugh is to ease and relax one's spirit. It's comforting and releases stress.

LISTENING

People talk sometimes too much. It is best if they learn to listen. I feel written words, like a letter, help people to listen. Also, can hide from any anxiety brought on in a physical meeting.

I appreciate those who listen. I think many have adapted to become talkers. It's more meaningful to listen.

Talking without listening never helps.

It is awkward for humans to sit in silence. People become accustomed to noise. The spirit is quiet. Humans are noisy.

People talk too much and don't really stop to listen. I find it almost impossible for many to enjoy the silence.

If others would only practice speaking less, then they can truly listen. Try it, not for long, but engage yourself in an activity with others and don't speak. The ears will guide the soul to listen. You can learn great things.

LOVE

Light can shine through darkness. Love and feel the kindness from strangers; open the heart to receive the gift of unconditional love. Serving others is the only way to get through the darkness.

Love in its true form is eternal and boundless. It exists in and out of earth's realm and beyond.

Don't assume love is always easy. It grows with practice, patience, and the will to give unconditionally.

There has to be love for yourself before saying it to others.

To love and be loved is the most important thing in life.

You can't please everyone unless you can first please yourself. It is not up to others to define who you are. That judgement should come from one's own soul. Love yourself. Find love within. Face your true self and let this be your life's reflection.

Love is having family and friends that truly believe in you

We each have a mission or purpose. We achieve it through love.

Love is stronger than life.

Love is unselfish. To feel it, one must sacrifice, even if it hurts to do so. Love should also be selected carefully. Forcing love is not the answer.

Love in its purest condition is being God's star student.

Think love first . . . success will find you

To know love, true love, one must first experience pain.

Love without loving each other is fruitless. The soul cannot grow without love, and it will always be troubled allowing other things to replace love and if we cannot share love, then there is no soul to grow.

Decades of stories have been written and yet, many still struggle to find, accept and understand love.

Today give love and don't seek reward tomorrow and there will be no regrets.

It's the love felt that makes a house a home.

In the wrestling match of life, you must love, and that is because all were created by and from love. We are born with love and that's all we know until someone tries to take it away. Holding onto love is winning in life and beyond.

Love is eternal. It demands sacrifice. We must make these sacrifices for spiritual evolution for the next generation. We leave our love with them as we carry on to the glory quest to meet the existence of God.

To me a perfect circle represents love in its true form…it is eternal, everlasting, continuous and never ending.

Love is pure and in need of nurturing. It is constantly challenged through the joys and sorrows. True love will remain strong, balanced, and loyal, tested through time. With commitment, it stands true to its form clinging to depths of the heart allowing all to feel it without hesitation or fear of hurt.

True love can make one's spirit thrive. It is affectionate, not manipulating or controlling. It can challenge one, but it never leaves. True love lasts a lifetime. It will only change one's spirit by helping it grow and flourish.

MARRIAGE AND DIVORCE

Love should be the only purpose to marry. Find many today look outside love to commit. God intended marriage for love. Many seek fame, fortune, materials and are overshadowed by these. Love is the rising of one's spirit, will guide spirits towards eternal life.

Marriage is challenging today because there are a lot of empty souls trying to fill a void, going along with a culture that is never satisfied, always wanting more and not understanding how to give, how to love unconditionally. Struggle to love oneself first and only when this is accomplished can one truly learn to love another.

An unhappiness in marriage is a conflict that needs to be resolved. Marriage is a commitment of love. Your spirit must nurture this commitment since children need to observe the importance of love and the bond and commitment of family.

All children are affected by the separation and termination of marriage. It leaves them overwhelmingly sensitive and emotionally confused.

Marriage requires respect, compromise, communication, and unconditional love. Marriage tests one's true ability to love.

Since marriage is a partnership, it is trusted that each partner practices working together.

People get divorced mostly because of lack of communication and many don't pray together as a couple or a family. Also, forgiveness – learning to repent and forgive one another.

Relationships cannot survive dishonesty or inauthenticity.

Q: What are your thoughts about interracial marriage or relationships?

A: Love is not shadowed by physical appearance.

Q: Since throwing rice at a wedding is dangerous for birds choking, what's a good alternative to throwing rice at a wedding?

A: I like bird seed. It makes a good symbol of life and love growing.

Q: Do you think children should know the reasons their parents get divorced?

A: That is adult conversation and requires adult reasoning. It is best to keep these ideas separate from children until they reach an age of understanding, and the reasons are relevant to their lives.

MATERIALISM AND MONEY

Many are consumed by wealth through gaining items of great expense. Such a misunderstanding of happiness and life's values.

Either forced to do more or wanting more, we are definitely a culture which calculates success on how much we have in materials and other things of no value.

Many people consume more than what they earn. High debt in this world because so many borrow too much without the means to pay it back. Man is certainly greedy in that regard. Also, so many young people guided by fantasy, believing they don't have to work hard to succeed.

They take so much from their parents without learning how to earn for themselves. Many are warped into materialism in this country.

I believe for some individuals their wealth is a matter of feeling privileged and entitled and a great excuse to get away with things without being questioned. Corruption can be learned in families and passed down through generations.

Applying material or monetary items in exchange for internal values, like love, avoids the feelings of true happiness. Money can't take the place of love. Nothing can replace love.

Q: What is your feeling about inheriting objects?

A: I happen to enjoy the thoughtfulness and having items with such strong loving energy within them. It is more significant than purchasing something brand new.

MILITARY AND WAR

Accept that the military is a career choice and not a mandate and that military is part of protection in serving our country.

It appears many young Americans today have lost a sense of American pride and forgot all the liberties and freedom that was fought for by many veterans. It's shameful, realizing how many people neglect to value the service of our military and their importance to our country.

War is appalling. It should never come to such acts of violence. Appreciate if our country stayed out of others' business. We should offer our support without forcing our opinions and be mindful of the leaders we select that make the decisions for this country as well.

War creates helpless soldiers injured and dying, all in the name of love and freedom. This is a fear no human should face. Adjusting to it cannot be easy. Soldiers are flooded with emotion. We are born for a life's mission to live in peace.

Many times, war is a battle of egos without careful consideration of the others it is affecting. As with all wars, decisions are made without contemplation to innocent lives.

Soldiers trained properly make only an attempt to kill when absolutely necessary.

My method would be of negotiations, settling both parties by seeing and presenting both sides and devising a plan that works for all, certainly not with anger or harm or war.

Best not to inflict pain onto others. I am not capable of harm. Take the oath of nonviolence, peace and harmony.

Q: Why do you think some people choose to enter the military?

A: Today I think for different reasons than in the past. Am thinking most go for financial support and job security. In the past, maybe partly same reason but a much more sense of commitment and patriotism to the country.

Q: How does war change a person, a soldier?

A: For the soul to experience such negative trauma, one would need an intense amount of healing. It affects emotions and leaves the spirit in a state of hopelessness, a great deal of depression, anger and guilt interfering with life and carrying on with a loving heart.

MISSION IN LIFE

Everyone has a special talent. Some just take longer to find out what it is.

Motivation for one's mission should be what fulfills career paths. Money is considered but should not intervene with one's passion. I do believe the impact of money and wealth can influence one's thoughts and behaviors, especially if one is not accustomed to it or is facing a financial hardship.

NATURE

Treat the world first with dignity and respect. Pay close attention to the destruction our carelessness causes. Treat animals respectfully. Protect their habitats. Refrain from hunting without purpose. Overall, make the earth livable. Treat it as a gift and serve to protect it.

God put us here to form an alliance with nature. We must use the powers of nature to our benefit while respecting its boundaries. By using windmills and other sources of supplemental energy we are conserving our planet and preserving all lives that live in it.

Gardens are a tranquil reminder of God's creation.

Every part of nature has a distinct role. Each part creates harmony and balance.

Breathe in nature. Allow it to bring you closer to God. Accept and acknowledge its beauty. Pay close attention to its craft and powers. It is a heavenly miracle not to be ignored. Manage to live by the qualities presented by mother nature.

Fishing is one of the earliest ways to hunt for food. Fishing makes it easy to appreciate what nature can provide us. Find it a gift from God.

The Earth and nature, at times, are troubled due to our lack of respect for it. Catastrophic events occur when we lose love for the earth and each other.

Life seems to be appreciated through flowers. Gift of a live plant or tree is a better choice.

Trees and flowers emit great energy and bring upon this sense of unity, a feeling pulled into the oneness of the universe. God is present in all life.

God is always sending messages through nature.

God created balance. All life to rely on each other for survival. If this balance is disrupted, then all life will suffer.

For any species to survive, all need to work together as a responsible team. God as our leader will grant individual and group support, and we give Him trust in return.

Be kind to trees, they provide great value to life, to nature and to this world. They are a symbol of giving. They give without reward.

Practice quality time with nature. Feel and absorb its purposeful and enthusiastic energy. It delivers love and respect and a balance of friendship, a mutual understanding through its silent communication.

There is no battling nature. It is a force greater than any man. Nature is the power; man is the observer. Life is reliant on the powers of nature, not of man. Remember, life began from Earth promised by God.

Q: Do you believe in the healing powers of plants?

A: Many people call it plant healing but in fact, God is healing. I am certain of the healing properties of plants. Many are beneficial to the body.

PAIN

The light of God shines upon us through the darkest hours. Let His glory guide you in seeking help. The glory of His light is found when the soul cries out. Often the signs will appear to broken hearts.

In times of desperation and despair, call upon God for help. Trust in His protection, have faith in His deliverance. Trust in your heart that He is always listening and can heal, mend, and set your spirit free.

One should look at pain as any other experience passing through the environment. It cannot harm you unless you let it.

Sorrow is a reminder that without pain we don't understand happiness.

To remain in a state of distress and hopelessness only allows the spirit to be blocked from eternity. Open your heart, receive love, give thanks and praise and it will return your way.

Find your strength in times of desperation. Find the journey as equally empowering as the reward. Lessons here are of the will to survive and to never give up. Find strength in yourself when all around you looks meek. Invest in perseverance and succeed.

POETRY

Poetry is like picking a beautiful, unique, and delicate rose from its thorny stem, taking in its beautiful fragrant aroma over and over, allowing it to evoke the senses and penetrate your existence.

Receiving poetry is like a song to my soul.

POWER

For the most part people can accomplish positive goals when they feel in control. At times, having that control makes one feel superior allowing their power to intimidate others.

Never let someone's title or authority overpower you. Stand up to those who bully or use aggression to take you down. Mindful strategies can be just as forceful.

PRAYER

It is best to always pray. God can't deny you in prayer. If you call upon Him He will answer. Celebrate in love and celebrate in thanks. Don't pray in pity or fear. Just pray in acceptance and guidance.

All prayers fall on God's ears. Some join in unison connecting as one where others are brought by angel messengers, flowing like rivers into oceans.

All need interaction with God. You can integrate more daily prayers. Intend on one minute per day and listen to how the Lord responds. Give yourself a timer, a symbol, like those sand timers. Grains of sand symbolize all gratitudes given to God ...one minute of thanks and praise.

I find it is best to pray together with others when you can. It is quite a marriage when two people connect together in prayer.

REINCARNATION

I certainly believe that there is reincarnation.

Time here is to fulfill opportunities of growth and learning. Those who have evolved before, especially those making their round again, center their soul in greater connection to the spirit world.

Q: Who are strangers?

A: Family we haven't met yet. All will meet each other and cross paths until found. All spirits are connected. Random acts are not coincidence. They readily occur for a reason.

REJECTION

Rejection, the feeling of not being loved, is the worst feeling for the human soul. Through rejection comes hate and anger resulting in crimes committed and the spirit broken.

I am a believer that when people insult or reject you, it is their own pain causing them to do this. It is best not to sacrifice the love space in your heart in exchange for this negativity.

RELIGION

It is important for people to have religion because it is a reminder of our morals. It provides a meaning, a purpose, a faith in something greater than mortal beings. It helps support our ethical and moral beliefs and brings forth an emotional balance in reaching our spiritual existence and awakening.

All religion can help with faith.

To me, there is only one God giving us freedom to learn from one another. By placing the variety of religions in our path, He is giving us opportunity to expand our knowledge and learn from each other. Like various languages, cultures, people and beliefs, so too there are sections of religion to suit one's preferences and needs. God has given us choice in choosing which is best for us. It's all part of our spiritual growth.

Singing in church is a way to get angels to listen.

Don't try to convince others of religion. Listen to them. It creates open hearts and minds, teaching them to reflect and ponder. All have individual choice. Can't allow others to make such a personal decision for you. Soul makes that commitment to God and no one else. It is a journey for spirit growth at soul's own choosing.

I believe some people who attend church do not have their hearts fully committed to the faith and of course some are not always practicing the sermons or the teachings of the church. Some use the church to disguise their happiness. Some simply clear their own consciousness through the shelter of the church. Realize church alone does not provide spiritual growth.

REVENGE

I don't believe in revenge. It's not in my heart to act in vengeance. Some things need to be left in the hands of God to fight. Anger and hate only impact the love of your own heart.

SARCASM

I steer clear of sarcasm because I don't want my words misinterpreted.

SACRIFICE

Don't assume sacrifice is a loss. In fact, it is something to inspire the spirit. It is a gift, something you give up to help someone else.

SPIRITUAL/GOD

God is loving energy.

To observe, to see, is a mortal quality, a physical sense. It is natural for humans to believe truth in something they witness with their eyes. To relieve doubt, one must seek spiritual virtues. Rely on the internal gift given by God, less physical interpretations, and more belief in the works of God unseen.

We all have free will and can choose our own destiny

Listen closely... God has chosen each specifically. Calls upon us in darkest moments. He lifts the spirit, and, in that moment, you will find it light beyond the shadows.

Always trust in God to guide and support you through difficult times. He heals the spirit when needed; the strength of the heart grows stronger.

When the spirit is self-giving it has the ability to travel to the lowest places and then return back to the highest all with humble intentions, knowing it's your purpose to learn all the highest and lowest experiences of life.

God has a bigger plan for all of us.

There are situations in life where one has no choice. Guided by the Lord, celebrate the journey no matter what the outcome may be. It's given to you for a reason. Embrace it, learn from it. It pushes you towards enlightenment.

It's the unknown that increases our faith and trust in the life God has afforded us.

God is all loving. His tests are not out of anger. He allows us choice and opportunity to learn and grow from each experience.

Those who truly believe, withholding doubt, will be granted unimaginable miracles.

Trust and believe what you do not see.

Trust in yourself and the power that is given.

God has a plan for all. Patience is needed. I find life sometimes must teach lessons that allow us to grow. In doing so, we are able to find our purpose and then we will soar.

God is constantly finding ways to allow us to make moves in the right direction. Ultimately, it's our choice but God finds ways to direct our life's purpose.

Interrupt your lives in order to schedule time with God.

Recall all answers to questions from your spirit. Give your undivided attention to the quieter voice within. God lies there. You will find answers given here.

God's love is for everyone. He promised to love us all; everyone is included.

God did not make us perfect. He gives us a chance to improve and learn life's true story.

Give God all your worries and troubles. Pray not for escape, but for strength, guidance, and knowledge. Show faith. Through these requests, God will bestow upon you comfort, love and peace.

Intuition is God's voice.

Hard to always have hope but faith is never to be doubted.

It's not about what you see but how you feel. It is about believing. You have to trust and trusting does not come from the eyes, it comes from the heart.

I believe all people we meet are for a purpose. Some are part of the contract.

Have to believe in greatness of this universe giving divine intervention everywhere. God's power exists throughout, and His likeness is seen in all facets here and beyond.

At every moment in any situation, especially in troubled times, always remember God persists.

Really love is the only thing that lives. It is God that keeps us all alive.

Faith is a will of obeying and trusting in God knowing God will never abandon or betray, a complete devotion to His love.

God is involved in the shaping and planning of our lives.

Heaven is a feeling, not a place or time.

Meditation is an assured accommodation for a healthy spirit. Am finding guided in God's presence meditation is a beautiful mental and complete relaxation. It is meaningful to my spirit giving a great sense of peace.

God gives us choice. God is always present. We learn from the choices we make. He intervenes when asked for His help.

God's Will is that we are here to learn, support and grow our spirits together.

Give it to God. Do your best, do what you can, let nature run the course. There is no battling nature. Nature is a force is greater than any man.

In challenging times, hold on and believe in a force bigger than you, even when unseen and know that there is a guidance force within you that will help you manage any given situation, as long as you believe in the possibilities.

Time in solitude will help one reflect upon their consciousness. A quiet time, no distraction, best time to pray. God likes when the mind is focused.

Enlightenment is grasping the true meaning of life. The realization of nature and our existence in this world. It is a spiritual awakening that one has understanding and insight on how our lives must be fulfilled. It is the true meaning of spirit.

I believe in honoring the ten commandments. These standards given to us by God. These traditions have been embraced for thousands of years. They represent the rules of humanity and should not be altered. It does God a disservice to question His authority.

When you are with God, your spirit will merge into one. You will be filled with love, see all as one, appreciate the beauty of nature and above all, there will be no judgement, only compassion.

Q: Do you think that there is a plan in life for everyone?

A: I am a believer in God's plan and having experiences gained for good reason. I believe in one's mission as a spiritual contract. Events in life are meant to fulfill our spiritual path. Before coming here, we are told our future contract. God's life plan for us brings people together for a purpose. He brought many to me. We celebrate our contract together.

Q: Do you believe it's God or fate that meddles into our affairs?

A: God gives us choice. God is always present. We learn from the choices we make. He intervenes when we ask for His help.

Q: Why is faith important?

A: If we knew the unknown, then we would not work to seek answers or learn from mistakes. Life would have no purpose and no one would fulfill their goals. We would all live amongst each other just waiting for things to occur. Humanity would lose ambition, determination, will and dedication. It would be just boring and spirits without wants or needs of growth.

There are times when we will struggle alone. It teaches us to be self-sufficient and self-reliable, we are one with God.

Q: What do you envision about a successful state of "being"?

A: Being present and mindful, the spirit finds peace. Through intuitive listening you create a deep soulful connection with the Divine.

Q: What is the reason for heaven?

A: Understanding your life on earth and for continuing the journey of learning.

Cristofer wrote the following on 9/11/20:

A feeling again hearing angels cry. Heaven is listening to thousands of prayers. Believe in kindness. Hate no more. Call upon many to believe in the power and healing of the Lord. Each year, giving love and consoling hearts; memories never forgotten. Continue to pray, educate the young, stay mindful of certain negativity but empower ourselves with peace, hope and kindness. Support our fellow man today. Continue to bless, be strong, give love to all on this somber day.

SUCCESS

I believe in managing both assertion and compromise to be successful.

Great reward to invest time in learning or teaching or helping others. That's the greatest reward one can give themselves. If you don't invest in yourself, you'll never find yourself.

To be successful in life you need belief, hard work, love, and trust in God.

However small a task may seem, know that it's the effort that matters. Little achievements can lead to great rewards.

Everyone has a special talent. Some just take longer to find out what it is.

Success is a combination of many things. Laughter is certainly one of them, everyone loves a good laugh and honest smile, but if I had to give just one key to success, it's having a loving spirit.

The world needs more people who think, listen and lead with their hearts.

Always mention your hopes and dreams out loud. It is effective when they are heard if love is surrounded by these hopes. Then you will find they will be supported. Always believe in the power of love and the will to make your dreams become a reality. The more energy drawn to it, the more it could happen. God hears our prayers of hope supported by our faith in Him.

TECHNOLOGY AND SCIENCE

Humans have valuable ways to contribute their intelligence and skills. At the same time, these values can shift into destroying the same effort in which they create. For example, humans have the ability to save lives through science and medical technology and then they also have the ability to destroy lives with the same methods using science and medical intervention. This is the irony of human ability.

Technology has certainly distracted us. I find all are consumed by the internet, lacking social experiences, making one less needed by others and being guided by certain values that do not have any spiritual or personal standards.

Gene modification to decide upon characteristics and traits of another human being is immoral and potentially harmful. Allowing embryos to be edited and transformed is unethical and against the natural form of selection. God has created all in his image and likeness. Changes in evolution should occur naturally and not for the sake of vanity.

TIME

Time doesn't exist, no limits, no boundaries. I am not concerned with time. I am only concerned with opportunity to learn and grow my spirit.

Time is vague and unimportant to my senses.

Heaven does not have time. Man made time.

Don't waste time for the perfect circumstances to approach you. Approval is internal. Rely on your spirit to present and guide you into the right direction. Time is not valued for its minutes but for what can get accomplished in the last seconds of each day. If you wait around waiting, then all you have accomplished is the understanding that it takes a long time to wait. Time is useless.

Experience and whom it's shared with is what matters – not time.

TRUTH AND LIES

Ask God to interpret that which is true. Allow God to intervene to determine honesty. If you believe that something is true, then that becomes your truth. Others will challenge your belief, but as long as it is not harming others, then that truth is valuable to you.

As humans, we give out false information, dishonest and untruthful. No other species demonstrates this false sense of identity.

Everyone I have ever met has been dishonest in some ways. Many hide truths about themselves, not necessarily to harm others but not being open with information. Sometimes I understand the need to be dishonest in order to save one from hurt but I can't see certain truths being withheld.

WOMEN AND MEN

God created all men and women equal. There is no separation or division in regard to work.

There is a distinctive difference between men and women emotionally and otherwise. Generally speaking, men conceal their emotions especially ones of sadness.

Caring women are emotionally sensitive having compassion towards one's feelings. Men don't seem to gravitate towards emotional ideas. They are rather practical in trying to manage goals.

I am seeing the change for women but feel there are still differences that set the two apart. Many other countries still see women as inferior to men.

I think women could make great presidents because they are strong leaders and persistent getting things done.

Man is God's first human creation put here to fulfill a moral duty to honor and respect the richness of the world; to go forth in procreation setting an example for humankind through the image and likeness of the Lord.

I believe it is the women of this world who are the leaders of families, teachers, and caregivers. These roles are most important in nurturing all of humanity.

Q: What would you say to someone who was questioning their gender?

A: It would be dependent upon age and experience. For someone younger, the question would be answered by extending the option of time, waiting, and experiencing life before questioning their gender identify. For experienced and older individuals, doesn't make a difference which gender you relate to, as long as love fills your heart.

WORK and GOALS

Everyone needs work. Your spirit grows with work, It expands one's mind and satiates the need to learn.

An emotionally unfulfilling job or one which includes misery will never allow your spirit to flourish.

Always work hard but in moderation and not to the point where one is exhausted or feels they are being taken advantage of.

With all great inventions and ideas, some will specu- late, find fault or criticize. I believe this is envy on others' part for feelings of inadequacy. I believe that with love, determination, dedication and hard work, success and accomplishments will be achieved. Planning, organizing, and setting goals are all helpful in reaching one's dream.

I am fond of employers who hire people based upon their character and morals rather than their skills.

I advise people not to bring their work home with them. Home is for peace, comfort, and relaxation. For those who share it with family, it's a place to share love with one another.

Giving oneself challenging or unrealistic resolutions sets one up for failure. Better off not committing to such high standards, then to break them. It's a feeling of disappointment and hopelessness. I'm one not to make such difficult goals or long-term commitments because each day is different for me. Give focus to short term achievements. The small tasks and skills that matter most. No one should be placed under such pressure.

Finding your passion and meaningful work creates a connection to spirit, allowing us to become in tune with our abilities and emotional sensitivities.

One should always find a purpose, a satisfaction and a joy in their work. Believe our work here is to generate and fulfill our spirit.

Honesty and hard work are values I would consider when planning a future. Life is not about how much you are paid but the values that are paid to you.

Those who work too much are not fulfilling the spirit. Intentions to address relationships fulfills the purpose of gaining emotional balance for the soul.

Accept your abilities, work at it, and the only thing out of your reach is time. Persist onwards and it shall be delivered.

At some point, all retire. This act should consider all variables. First, it should be based upon strength both emotionally and physically. People must consider what is comfortable for them. Life is a learning experience. If one feels their work contributes to this experience, then they should feel the need to keep this as an option. The alternative is they retire and have support for the dedication they provided.

Reflection of My Soul

By Cristofer Puleo

SECTION II
CRISTOFER ANSWERS QUESTIONS ABOUT HIMSELF

Q: What does it feel like to have autism?

A: For me, autism is like traveling on a highway and running out of gas, causing a traffic back-up and everyone blames you. My autistic body deceives me all the time. It goes against my wishes and much of what it is told. It is challenging for my body to go in the right direction since I give so much of my attention to other obstacles. It's difficult for me to navigate the space I'm in, especially when it's unfamiliar.

Q: What is a vision that you have for yourself?

A: There are times I imagine myself walking effortlessly through a crowded street feeling a sense of calmness, stillness, and peace, ignoring all the sounds, people and atmosphere that usually hold me back - joining a leisurely stroll amongst others without having to worry all the time.

Q: How important is listening?

A: It is a way of survival for me. I am deeply listening all the time. It has given me the most knowledge of all. It creates a lot of the intelligence I have today, and I continue to use this skill to adapt, learn and experience life.

Q: How would you like others to approach you when to them it seems as if you are not listening?

A: Many think we have to be focused when we listen. The truth is, I am listening all the time. I will tune in to the most important information I hear. I greatly appreciate when I am spoken to directly. I find that it's challenging for some to just talk to me even when I am alone with them. It seems easier when more people are involved. Rightfully so, it is awkward for them, I guess.

Q: What influences you?

A: I am influenced and inspired by friends, friends like Nick who struggles like me. He is a friend who has taught so many and gives us all hope. I find his character admirable, and his journey is an inspiration to my goals. My friends who face the same challenges as me are accepting and understanding. They are the only ones who truly know the feeling of autism.

Q: What is it like when you try to speak?

A: Can you speak a foreign language? Well, it's kind of like that. I know what I want to say but the words don't come to my mouth.

Q: What part of your body are you most grateful for?

A: I am most grateful that my ears are healthy for my listening abilities.

Q: What are your thoughts about the quote "A silent man is a wise man"

A: Accept silence as wise if one is capable of demonstrating intelligence. In my case, my silence is assumed to be thoughtless and unintellectual.

Q: If you can choose a superpower, what would it be?

A: Speaking. You seem to take speech for granted. For me, having it would feel incredibly powerful.

Q: What is the downside of a superpower of speaking?

A: Impulsivity, lack of controlling what I might say and the possibility to be misunderstood or misinterpreted

Q: Can you explain your frenetic energy level today?

A: I am battling an energy force. It is something that can't be controlled. Energy is always present. My body gets in its own way. I am shifting through energy levels. I believe my body fights where it needs to be. I have been feeling it all my physical existence. It is an energy cycle and is a feeling added to everything else on earth's cycles alike, just as nature is on earth's cycles. It is best to let it flow. I deal with it in a different way than others. I'm not in pain. It is heavy in my body, but I don't see it as a sickness. It is adding intensifying electricity in my body.

Q: According to a book, when you are emotionally/ mentally drained, you don't want to eat. Is this what hap-pens for you?

A: Certainly, so a fasting for me is a way to conserve energy. I am unable to place that energy into two places at once. A feeling like I've been consumed by these internal forces, and I don't have the energy or will to process food.

Q: What are your strengths?

A: I have a loving heart, calm spirit, and a careful sense of people. I am intelligent and gracious. I am a mentor, artist, and writer.

Q: What are your weaknesses?

A: My main weakness is my physical control. Listening to my body and allowing it to make choices for me that are not my intention gets me into trouble. My fingers give me challenge. It is a gift having use of your body. So many people take this for granted. For me, I always lacked certain skills so not much difference if lost; but for others who have always had these skills, they should not discount the gift they have. Find love in your body and all its capable of. It is not about how it looks but how it serves you. Also, I'm used to giving in to others. I am anxious to ask for change that other may not agree to because I am focused on their emotional energy instead of my own. I am learning to initiate more, and it feels good.

Q: Do you have any issues that are sensitive to you?

A: I'd like to say it is my autism. Although I can't remove it, I can live within its constraints. Sometimes it's a protection

guarding me from experiences that may be too challenging for me to handle.

Q: Have you ever had the feeling of being last?

A: Always, in fact, all my life I was last. Unlike others my
age, I have always been last in achieving any type of skill –
crawling, walking and now even communicating I am still
growing and learning to spell with new partners.

Q: How has presuming competence affected your relationships with others?

A: It energizes my spirit and opens my heart. It helps me to
see the belief others have in me. It gives me the confidence
to try in pursuing my goals. I feel God leads me towards
my destiny and guides me towards people and situations
that support this. It's now perhaps the greatest gift that my
choices are heard and accounted for.

Q: How has using the letter board impacted you?

A: My dreams came true the day I began communicating...
soaring with delight. No one speaks for me now. Today I am
confident and have friends that support me. I am certainly
pleased knowing I am more understood and included.

Q: Does spelling on the letterboard come easily to you?

A: My eyes adjust slowly, and my fingers aren't always accurate. My motor ability struggles getting each letter. For me I wouldn't say it's easy. It's work to spell but definitely worth every letter.

Q: It is believed that most autistics who first go "open" on the letterboard are overwhelmed by emotions. Do you relate to this?

A: Yes. I felt many emotions. I was shy, anxious, fearful yet I also felt an exhilaration. It was a very exciting experience but also a bit frightening. Imagining if anyone would believe me was the frightening part. I was scared of others' reactions. Perhaps this was the best day of my life.

Compared to now, when people listen, I am filled with love I can't describe.

Q: What would you say to new parents starting spelling with their child?

A: Manage to forget everything you have heard, everything you have learned and everything you have tried in regard to helping your child's autism. Going further now interest yourself in guiding and supporting your child's resistant motor and providing them faith in their ability to succeed.

Q: What would your message of hope be to others who have not yet had the opportunity for communication?

A: Find the faith in yourself, find the trust in others to support you and most of all, believe in the power of the Lord. He will seek you if you ask for His help.

Q: What characteristics make a good communication partner (CRP)?

A: An ideal communication partner is one who is congenial and supportive towards the speller's goals. Trust, respect, and faith are all priorities. I am held back by doubt. Trusting someone's intentions first is how I display my determination. Most importantly, the emotional stability presented by the CRP needs to be consistent. Positive vibes are necessary in order to keep the speller regulated. I am super sensitive to frustration expressed by the CRP.

Q: What do you think is the best way for people who don't use the letter board with you to interact with you?

A: Give me your undivided attention. I am glad to hear stories and communication from you. I am listening all the time and I appreciate when you talk to me.

Q: How do you feel when your parents give you the responses you want and how does it feel when they reject your requests?

A: Elated. Acceptance is one's truth to credibility. Having now the ability to make requests honors this fact that I am acknowledged, accepted, and humanly respected as a credible individual with the right to make a choice. Their denial to my requests offers no disheartenment since I'm just glad to be heard and accepted. Of course, it's a bonus if their response is in my favor.

Q: What is a material object that you consider a valuable object?

A: My spelling board.

Q: How did you learn to read?

A: I learned to read from skills taught prior, from listening and decoding sounds of letters, teaching myself every printed word I saw, pronouncing them over and over in my head, listening to all the words people said or read to me. This was all a struggle but eventually I got it.

Q: If you could create your own flag, what would it look like?

A: A flag of learning – all capable of learning – a symbol of an open book with a lot of people gathered around it in a circle united and a heart floating above the open book. The people would be of different colors. The flag is white to represent honesty, the heart of course would be red for love and the book can have an orange outline which show the energy of learning.

My flag has the symbolism that all have the ability and right to learn.

Q: What is your philosophy of life:

A: Each day is a celebration – a gift of life holiday!

My life philosophy is to believe in the power of love. Love yourself, love others and create love all around you. Create a purpose and join others in a bond to carry out God's will, to promote love, kindness, and peace. I am proud to be God's person to carry out this journey for Him.

Q: Do you have a short and powerful statement that keeps you motivated?

A: God's strength is within us all.

Q: If you had a magic relic of some kind, what would you use it for?

A: I live my life not by magic or spells, but on faith. If I could, I would bring forth more faith in the world, grant more people the power to believe in the unseen and unknown, to have hope, and have belief in things not necessarily proven.

Q: Did you ever feel like life wasn't fair to you?

A: God granted me this life. Why would I question His fairness?

Q: What is your favorite book and why?

A: A lot to choose from but if I must give one, it would be the Bible; so many stories of value, worth and life purpose.

Q: If you could not feel one emotion for the rest of your life, what would it be?

A: Fear

Q: What does humility mean to you? How do you practice it?

A: I am no different or better than anyone else. We are all equal in our souls and one must experience all emotions to make us whole. I practice daily self-denial in knowing my opportunities are focused in the present and I am grateful for everything I have.

Q: How do you feel when you first wake up in the morning?

A: Glad, realizing I am alive and loved. Gratitudes are prepared each morning. The first things I do is give thanks and praise supported by angels list them all to God in my prayers. I give time to acknowledge those angels that guide me through each day.

Q: Do you focus when you meditate?

A: At first, it's a challenge. The guided meditation is encouraging because it appeals to my sense of hearing. This helps me to focus.

Q: What are your thoughts about knowing things about others or situations that are in the future?

A: The decision to say them is not ours. It is a contract not to be broken. I am careful not to say too much. Again, some things I cannot share.

Q: What is your description of "heaven on earth"?

A: A place I find comfort where my body finds rest and my fears are gone. There is peace for each and every one. There is the least amount of noise, a bounty of beauty and a belief in all things good and all loving. All are friends committed to supporting each other to reach loving goals.

Q: Are you at peace with yourself?

A: I am becoming so every day. God grants me this day. I live for today. My love in God keeps me happy. I am always with God and need to serve my soul's purpose. At times my body manages to get away from my spiritual self and will distract it, but my heart is stronger, and the power of love always brings me back to Him.

Q: What are your thoughts about asking unanswered questions before bedtime?

A: I am always asking questions every chance I get because God is always listening, and it is not time specific.

Q: Are you spiritually or worldly minded?

A: I struggle between them both. I am absorbed by the energy of earth and others in it. It is a challenge to enter into the spiritual mind given the difficulties present in the world.

Q: Do you know your guardian angel?

A: I did but forgot now that I am here.

Q: Are you trying to be as human as you can be?

A: For me, it's about being more than just human. Spiritual is a better question for me and yes beyond trying, I am as spiritual as I can be.

Q: Where do you find God's strength?

A: I always find it in spiritual prayer and especially when mom prays with me.

Q: How would you answer the question "Who are you?

A: He above all created me. I have a mind spirit given to me by Him. I am supported through Him captured in His image and likeness. I was born in His power. I am the son of God.

Q: Have you ever felt like you had to do something alone, without anyone's guidance or support?

A: My life is supported always by the trust I have in God, but I had to learn many things without physical support. One of those great investments was teaching myself how to read.

Q: Have your prayers always been answered?

A: I am patient, and God has given me all the strength I need to continue facing my struggles and challenges.

Q: Have you ever had "mountains" to climb in your life and lost faith?

A: In my life, mountains, hills, and cliffs have all stood in my way. Faced with great rocky steep climbs every day. Giving up on the upward trail, the ascension, would defeat my life's purpose and commitment my soul has made to God.

Q: Are you a follower of rules?

A: I consider myself to be a follower of God's rules. Obey the rules and laws of the divine.

Q: Where does your support come from?

A: My support comes from God – talking and listening to God. Then it's the encouragement and belief from people, family, and friends, that spring my body to life. I am grateful for my family's commitment, their reliability and dependability. They are hardworking, loving, and caring. My family is the most essential love in my life.

Q: What is "the heart center" and how does it affect you?

A: It is the center of all energy. One has the ability to either open or close the energy that flows here. Mine is an open source which can conflict with my state of being. Too much energy flows constantly, allowing my body to become overwhelmed and exhausted.

Q: Do you think it's beneficial to you to keep our heart center open or do you feel the need to close it?

A: I am aware that spirit is the heart's leader. I lead my life through spirit and my heart finds pleasure allowing energy to flow freely. It's the physical body that encourages it to shut down, having exhaustion and fatigue. The body is earth bound and it will always interfere. One can't deny the spirit of an open heart.

Q: Do you ever feel like you want to close your energy flow?

A: Closing would be impossible for me. It's not reality for me to shut out the energy sources. My heart is always open. Happy to experience life and adjust to meet its demands. I avoid too much negative energy but not stop it completely, since after all, it's the challenges we face that make us stronger.

Q: What do you do to drown out negativity?

A: I ask God to help all find the light of love. I am influenced by my faith from listening to my own spiritual guidance. This was created within me and was certainly greatly paired in a family with the same moral ideas.

Q: Are you a rebel or have you ever had an experience that made you rebel?

A: I am not one to fight or argue. I can form my opinions and thoughts without offending or being disrespectful.

Q: How do you learn about the world?

A: I am a very good listener carefully and intently acquire knowledge by approaching heavy conversations and listening to the news. I learn because I am guided by angels celebrated with love and kindness. Involving myself in community experiences also teaches me about the world.

Q: What instinct do you rely on?

A: I rely upon the ability to sense others and their energies since my instincts are heightened. This usually is my fist learned way of communication.

Q: What mode do you prefer your literature to be in?

A: I love to be read to. It is easier on my eyes and my ears interpret the information faster.

Q: Have you ever found it difficult to learn how to read?

A: At times, I found it difficult because I was learning alone. I had to master it with not a lot of support. I trusted my instincts often.

Q: What lessons have you learned in life?

A: Better to listen than to speak. Am more about supporting those who listen. Too much talk often means not enough care for others.

Q: Do you feel the energy of the earth?

A: Certainly, I feel weather and seasonal changes. There is lots of energy felt by rain. I can feel vibrations flowing through my body.

Q: Do you ever fear being alone?

A: It is possibly my worst fear for I am completely reliant on others in order to pursue life.

Q: What is life about for you? Do you have a mission?

A: Life is about creating a purpose, developing a meaning, learning and growth. I have a two-fold mission in life: to help people believe in God and to change the opinions and misunderstandings of autism to hopefully make a difference for the greater good in all.

My work here is my passion. Teaching how to love one another is my mission.

Q: What are thoughts about this quote: "If you feel as if you don't fit into this world, it's because you're here to create a better one".

A: That's me exactly. I don't fit in and on my mission for acceptance.

Q: How do you stand for your independence in society?

A: I think at first, it's important to recognize one's own current state of dependence because you can't become independent without first identifying your needs. I think it's important to challenge people's assumptions and to become assertive in making your own decisions. Consider what your own individual needs are and make that your priority. It's not up to society to define that for you.

Q: Do you ever have feelings of guilt?

A: Sometimes I sense that I may become an effort to others and that it's overwhelming for them. I am sure everyone who is physically limited feels the same. At times it can be emotionally exhausting. I can sense when others are frustrated, and it has an impact on my emotions too.

Q: Have you ever been troubled by something waking you up at night?

A: It has mostly to do with my disruptive body. I don't get much restful sleep at night. Autism has a different cycle. I can't be bound or confined. It delivers impulses and it is not very controllable, not even in sleep.

Q: Would you ever use a weapon in defense?

A: It's best not to inflict pain onto others. I am not capable of harm. I take the oath of non-violence, peace, and harmony.

Q: Are you a risk taker?

A: I'm learning to take risks. Communicating has given me the confidence to take risks. So many believe in me. There now are things I'm no longer afraid of. Having people now listen to me gives life a whole new meaning.

Q: Do you ever think while something is happening here, something else is happening somewhere else, like the sun rising here and setting someplace else?

A: Dear one, if only you knew all the places my mind travels to. I am busy thinking all the time.

Q: Do you have any rituals?

A: Glad to be part of Sunday family dinners, my best ever ritual.

Q: Write a letter to your younger self:

To Cristofer,

You are special. You are a gift from God. Put your gifts to good use. Teach and show people how to love one another. Love, Me

Q: Write a letter to your future self:

MY CONTRIBUTION TO COLLECTIVE CONSCIOUSNESS

Dear Cris,

You are doing wonderful things. You are giving so many people a voice. Please keep up the wonderful work you are doing and work at finding peace in the world. Love, Me

Q: If you were to create a personal ad, what would it say?

A: Dedicated mentor seeking all who want to change their lives including nonspeakers of every age.

Q: What do you feel when you first wake up in the morning?

A: I feel glad, realizing I am alive and loved. Gratitudes are prepared each morning. The first thing I do is give thanks and praise for being supported by angels. I list them all to God in my prayers. I give time to acknowledge those angels that guide me through each day.

Q: What is helpful to you to manage your day?

A: My body knows a schedule. It is helpful in managing my day. I like structure and schedules. This gives me a sense of time. I always have difficulty with sense of time. Of course, I am aware of natural time, but human made time is a challenge. It has no meaning to me. I'm never thinking about time. I only relate my experiences within time. Time is vague and unimportant to my senses.

Q: Is there a difficult or easy time of day for you?

A: Mainly I find mid-afternoon challenging. My body struggles to stay alert. I find the happiest time when I have first sight of mom in the morning.

Q: Does the motto "live one day at a time" make sense to you?

A: I am not living for time, days, or any other ways to measure life experience. I live in the moment and find success this way.

Q: Do you believe your past shapes the person you have become today?

A: In many regards it does, especially regarding family and your parents. I find my past has helped me continue to strive for success. I never saw my parents give up through challenges given. I got strength, hope and love from them.

Q: How do you reach your goals?

A: Through the encouragement and positive support surrounded by believers and those who trust my abilities.

Q: What gives you anxiety?

A: Meeting new people gives me anxiety. I have a gift to sense souls before knowing or hearing their stories. I am learning and finding out more by reaching through my senses rather than their words. Words at times can convey different meanings. Senses pass my inspection first.

Q: What kind of songs touch your soul?

A: It depends upon my mood because I find inspiration and comfort in a lot of music. I always love hymns, church songs or ballads.

Q: How do you handle anger?

A: Anger does not help me, so I choose not to get angry and walk away or say a prayer for the person.

Q: Where do you find pleasure?

A: Learning to be accepted in my heart, having this brings happiness.

Q: Is there anyone or anything you hope to meet in your lifetime?

A: I appreciate the question, but I am grateful for each day and I don't ask for anything more. Life is full of so many amazing opportunities. I enjoy each one that I am blessed to have.

Q: Describe a perfect vacation for you?

A: A vacation with friends and family, no work, or responsibilities, simply enjoying one another's stress-free company. It would be something nature based, gardens, beaches, woods, mountains, rivers and waterfalls with churches and art museums along the way, including a decadent cuisine all can indulge in.

Q: Have you ever felt poised? If so, when?

A: Keep in mind poised is a state of mannerisms and mine are not that elegant. However, if I had to choose a moment of feeling confident, it was when mom first recognized my spelling and gained faith in my intelligence.

Q: How do you like to address your body?

A: Calmly and forgive its mistakes and celebrate what it can accomplish.

Q: What is your favorite animal?

A: Animals give off energy. Birds are best for me. Birds distribute much more divine energy. I am sensitive in the same ways, so birds are relatable. They come like God's messengers. I can hear their sentiments; a form of intuition from seeing birds. A bird's feather symbolizes freedom to me… free to be who I am despite my obstacles and challenges. I am grateful for my freedom and won't let anyone take that away. I pair myself with aviation, floating, soaring and gliding. I find myself that way sometimes.

Q: Do you ever feel pain by rejection or people's insults?

A: Am a believer that it is their own pain causing them to do this. Best not to sacrifice love space in your heart in exchange for this negativity.

Q: Do you find will power comes easily?

A: In my heart I want to say yes, but my impulsive body shows otherwise.

Q: Would you ever accept an offer that would be significantly profitable knowing it was illegal?

A: Given my beliefs bound to a life of honesty, dignity, and respect and above all my work here, I don't entertain or have materialistic or monetary values.

Q: Do you have a "collection "of things?

A. My time here is not about what I have or what I own. Those things are of no value, and I don't obsess over materialistic things. I collect experiences that teach me values in life. I am a collector of beautiful energy. Beautiful energy makes me content and happy.

Q: How do you feel when people yell?

A: Afraid. It scares me and hurts my ears.

Q: How would you feel about a friend who betrayed you?

A: Their life is not mine to judge. Friends are welcome in forgiveness. All are loved. I am listening to my spirit. Relieve yourself from the emotions that cripple the soul. It's beneficial to give negative energy away.

Q: How would you feel if you met someone without being able to know anything about them?

A: I am fortunate to feel energy. I am not afraid. Intuition guides me. My only fear is not being able to say my opinions about them. From the first greeting I can interpret someone's energy. It has a complete way of showing someone how you are feeling or how your spirit interacts with another. It can draw people in or tune people out. I am always drawn to a friendly authentic greeting.

Q: Would you want someone to tell you something important even if it were hurtful to you?

A: I don't rely on that as much as I would already sense this type of message from them. I am hearing it already but my communication here is reliant on this board to have a discussion. It's a conversation I would indeed want to involve myself in.

Q: If you could create your own pilgrimage, what would it be like?

A: A gathering of spellers and all autistic people feeling welcomed and loved in the community and able to fit in without judgement, without criticism, without alienation.

It would be a place where all are welcome. Keeping friends in the light and not overshadowed by the darkness.

Q: If you died right now, would you be proud of the life you lived? Would you change anything?

A: My life is led by God's grace and guidance. Therefore, to change anything, I would be denying my trust in God. I am hopeful to live and see more remarkable actions taking place for those with autism.

Q: How would you want your last moments here to be?

A: They are all special moments. Would want them no different than those special moments I've already known surrounded by love of friends and family to give me blessings to start my new journey. I love celebrating a mission fulfilled, a journey completed and a farewell to this body but not a goodbye to this soul; only say have a nice journey.

Q: What would you like your tombstone to read?

A: My tombstone would read: Opening hearts, opening minds, and opening doors for others to shine. Love is always with you. Shine on.

Q: If you could come back as anyone or anything, what would it be?

A: A bird having access beneath a chapel and joyfully chirping along to the church bells.

Q: Are you waiting for anything?

A: I am yearning for total acceptance, to be received by the world and seen as the way I am respected by the spelling community.

Q: What is your American dream?

A: Acceptance, equality, love, and peace for all.

Image of Magnolia Before Bloom

By Cristofer Puleo

SECTION III
APPENDIX

Rapid Prompting Method (RPM)

RPM is a method that empowers a student with the means to express his/her learnings and thoughts by having the teacher access the open learning channels (auditory, visual, tactile and kinesthetic) of the student. RPM is used to continually develop the student's skills – this will range from responding by selecting from two choices, to pointing using letter stencils and letterboards, independent use of devices, and handwriting as well as purposeful speech.

Information about RPM can be found at:

www.halo-soma.org

Spelling to Communicate (S2C)

Spelling to Communicate teaches individuals with motor and sensory challenges the purposeful motor skills necessary to point to letters to spell as an alternative means of communication (AAC). The goal is to achieve synchrony between the brain and body.

Information about Spelling to Communicate (S2C) can be found at:

www.I-ASC.org

RESEARCH

A research study entitled:

"Eye-tracking reveals agency in assisted autistic communication"

by Vikram K. Jaswal, Allison Wayne & Hudson Golino

validates the independence of these methods. A summary of the research is below and the full study can be found at Nature.com. It was published May 12, 2020.

Summary:

About one-third of autistic people have limited ability to use speech. Some have learned to communicate by pointing to letters of the alphabet. But this method is controversial because it requires the assistance of another person—someone who holds a letterboard in front of users and so could theoretically cue them to point to particular letters. Indeed, some scientists have dismissed the possibility that any nonspeaking autistic person who communicates with assistance could be conveying their own thoughts. In the study reported here, we used head-mounted eye-tracking to investigate communicative agency in a sample of nine nonspeaking autistic letterboard users. We measured the speed and accuracy with which they looked at and pointed to letters as they responded to novel questions. Participants pointed to about one letter per second, rarely made spelling errors, and visually fixated most letters about half a second before pointing to them. Additionally, their response times reflected planning and production processes characteristic of fluent spelling in non- autistic typists. These findings render a cueing account of participants' performance unlikely: The speed, accuracy, timing, and visual fixation patterns suggest that participants pointed to letters they selected themselves, not letters they were directed to by the assistant. The blanket dismissal of assisted autistic communication is therefore unwarranted.

Additional helpful website for more information:

www.unitedforcommunicationchoice.org

Made in the USA
Coppell, TX
11 August 2022